ANIMAL BABIES

by Margaret Shanley

Consultant: Beth Gambro
Reading Specialist, Yorkville, Illinois

BEARPORT
PUBLISHING

Minneapolis, Minnesota

Teaching Tips

Before Reading

- Briefly discuss animal life cycles. Babies are born, they grow, and they have their own babies.

- Look through the glossary together. Read and discuss the words.

- Go on a picture walk, looking through the pictures to discuss vocabulary and make predictions about the text.

During Reading

- Encourage readers to point to each word as it is read. Stop occasionally to ask readers to point to a specific word in the text.

- If a reader encounters an unknown word, ask them to look at the rest of the page. Are there any clues to help them understand?

After Reading

- Check for understanding.

  ▸ What are some things baby sloths do during the first few weeks? What about after that?

  ▸ Find a place in the book that tells you what a baby sloth eats.

  ▸ Look at page 22. What did you learn about baby sloths from reading this book?

- Ask the readers to think deeper.

  ▸ Other than size, what is one thing that is different about baby sloths and adult sloths?

  ▸ What is one thing that is similar about baby and adult sloths?

Credits:
Cover, © accarvalhophotography/Shutterstock; 3, © Perla Sofia/Shutterstock; 5, © KenCanning/iStock; 6-7, © Suzi Eszterhas/Minden Pictures; 8, © Katie Louise Marshall/Shutterstock; 9, © Suzi Eszterhas/Minden Pictures; 10-11, © Oyvind Martinsen-Panama Wildlife/Alamy Stock Photo; 12, © ATTILA KISBENEDEK/Getty Images; 13, © Nate Gautsche/Getty Images; 14, © Damocean/iStock; 15, © KenCannin/Getty Images; 16-17, © Kristel Segeren/Shutterstock; 18, © FBF_BsAs/iStock; 20-21, © Urs Hauenstein/Shutterstock; 22, © worldswildlifewonders/Shutterstock; 23TL, © Nacho Such/Shutterstock; 23TR, © Alastair Munro/Shutterstock; 23BL, © Phil West/Shutterstock; 23BC, © ChisholmJA/Shutterstock; 23BR, © kungverylucky/Shutterstock.

Library of Congress Cataloging-in-Publication Data

Names: Shanley, Margaret, 1972– author.
Title: Baby sloths / by Margaret Shanley.
Description: Bearcub books edition. | Minneapolis, Minnesota: Bearport
  Publishing Company, [2021] | Series: Animal babies | Includes
  bibliographical references and index.
Identifiers: LCCN 2020015854 (print) | LCCN 2020015855 (ebook) | ISBN
  9781642809602 (library binding) | ISBN 9781642809671 (paperback) | ISBN
  9781642809749 (ebook)
Subjects: LCSH: Sloths—Infancy—Juvenile literature.
Classification: LCC QL737.E2 S53 2021 (print) | LCC QL737.E2 (ebook) |
  DDC 599.3/131392—dc23
LC record available at https://lccn.loc.gov/2020015854
LC ebook record available at https://lccn.loc.gov/2020015855

Copyright © 2021 Bearport Publishing Company. All rights reserved. No part of this publication may be reproduced in whole or in part, stored in any retrieval system, or transmitted in any form or by any means, electronic, mechanical, photocopying, recording, or otherwise, without written permission from the publisher.

For more information, write to Bearport Publishing, 5357 Penn Avenue South, Minneapolis, MN 55419.

Printed in the United States of America.

Contents

It's a Baby Sloth!

A sloth hangs in a tree.

She is **upside down**.

She just had her baby hanging this way!

Her **newborn** opens its little eyes.

A mother sloth carries her baby.

The baby **reaches** its legs out to the hair on its mother's belly.

Hold on!

The baby is very small.

It is about as heavy as a baseball.

It has long claws on its feet.

Claw

The baby hangs on its mom.

It cannot do anything by itself.

The mother carries the baby with her.

They move slowly through the trees.

The baby sloth drinks milk from its mother's body.

Soon, the baby eats leaves, too.

It learns to eat by licking its mother's mouth!

Yum!

A baby sloth sleeps a lot.

It can sleep for most of the day!

The mother takes her baby to the ground once a week.

There, she will pee and poop!

Then, she climbs back up to hang in the trees for another week.

After a few months, the sloth is bigger.

It can leave its mother.

It hangs in trees on its own.

When the sloth is a few years old, it is an **adult**.

Now it can **mate** and have babies of its own!

The Baby's Body

Head

Eye

Claw

Leg

Glossary

adult a grown-up

mate to come together to have young

newborn a baby that was just born

reaches stretches out the arms to touch something

upside down with the top at the bottom and the bottom at the top

Index

Read More

Kenney, Karen Latchana. *Sloths (Blastoff! Readers: Animals of the Rain Forest).* Minneapolis: Bellwether Media (2021).

Murray, Julie. *Sloths (Abdo Kids, I Like Animals!).* Minneapolis: Abdo Kids (2017).

Learn More Online

1. Go to **www.factsurfer.com**
2. Enter "**Baby Sloths**" into the search box.
3. Click on the cover of this book to see a list of websites.

About the Author

Margaret Shanley once traveled to Costa Rica just to see the sloths!